Idaho State Capitol

Boise

Jane Moorman

There is a saying, "It was a Friday night and it seemed like a good idea at the time." That sums up the beginning of the State Capitols Project.

When I told my brother of my idea of photographing state capitols, he said, "You do know there are 50 states and two of them you can't drive to."

Each capitol has its own unique beauty that reflects the state's personality when it was built.

Jane Moorman, photographer

Idaho's Statehouse

When architect J.E. Tourtellotte designed the neoclassical style Idaho Capitol building, he believed that "the great light of conscience must be allowed to shine and by its interior illumination make clear the path of duty." For Tourtellotte, light was a metaphor for an enlightened and moral state government.

He incorporated this belief into the design using light shafts, skylights, and reflective marble surfaces to capture natural sunlight and direct it to the interior.

The original design created an architecturally pleasing building that incorporated the materials and technologies of the day into a working capitol.

This desire to use natural resource continues today with the use of geothermal water to heat the building. The hot water is tapped and pumped from a source 3,000 feet underground. Idaho's Capitol is the only one in the United-States heated this way.

Construction on the building's dome and central area began in 1905 and was completed in 1912. The legislative wings were constructed during 1919-1920.

The 2009 renovations preserved, restored, rehabilitated and expanded the original building.

Underground atrium wings were added to accommodate larger, more spacious legislative hearing rooms.

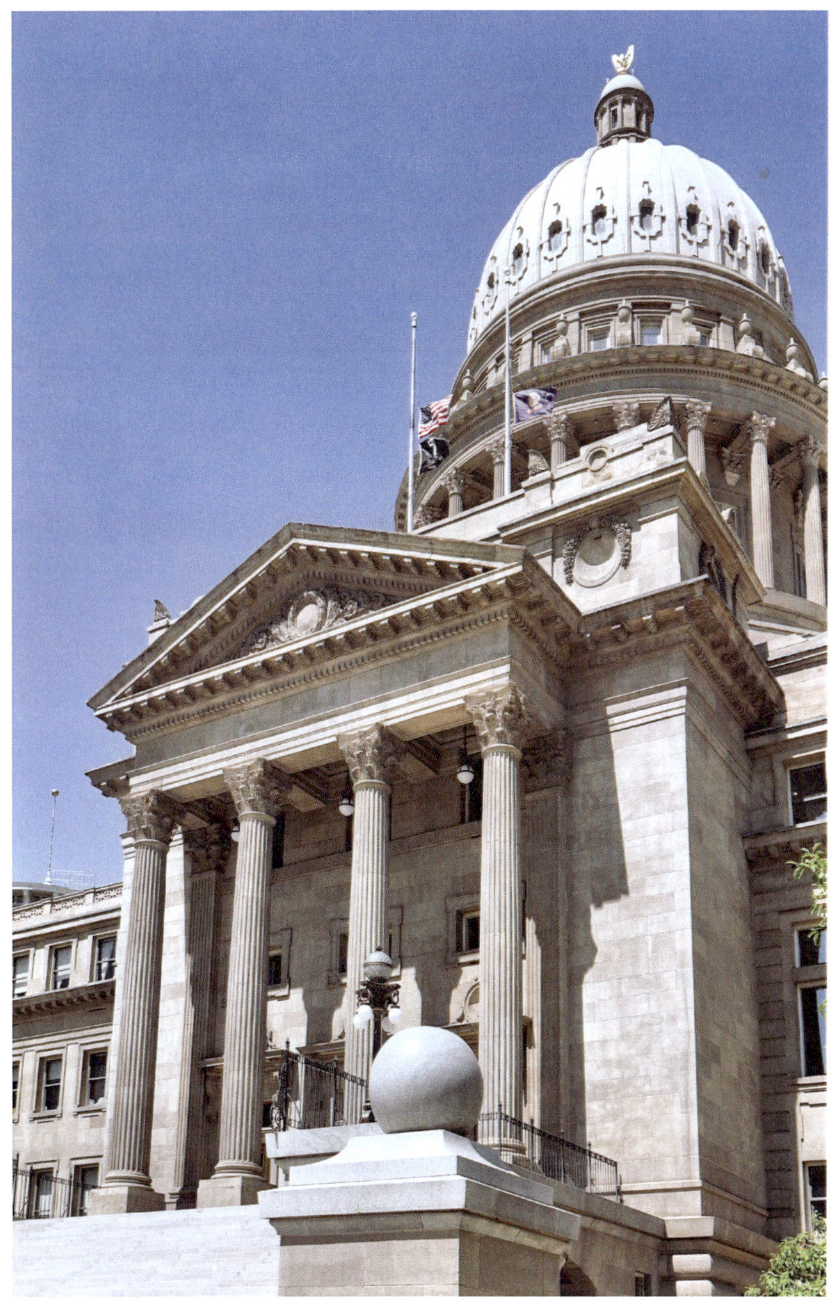

Golden Eagle

Standing spread winged atop of the dome is a 5-foot 7-inches eagle made of copper. In 2005, as part of the exterior restoration, it received a new gilding of gold leaf.

From the ground to the eagle atop the dome, the Idaho Capitol Building rises 208 feet.

Exterior of the building is made of sandstone taken from Table Rock, near Boise, and Vermont granite.

Convicts from the old Idaho Penitentiary were responsible for transporting the 10-ton sandstone blocks from the quarry.

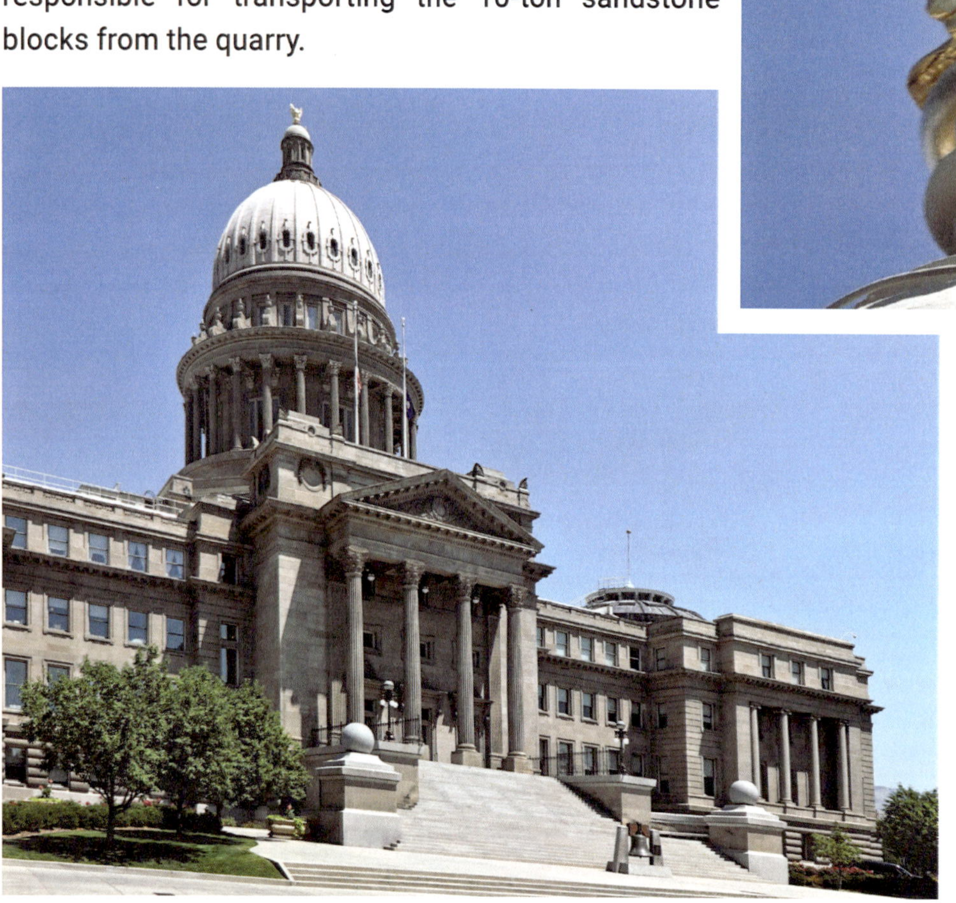

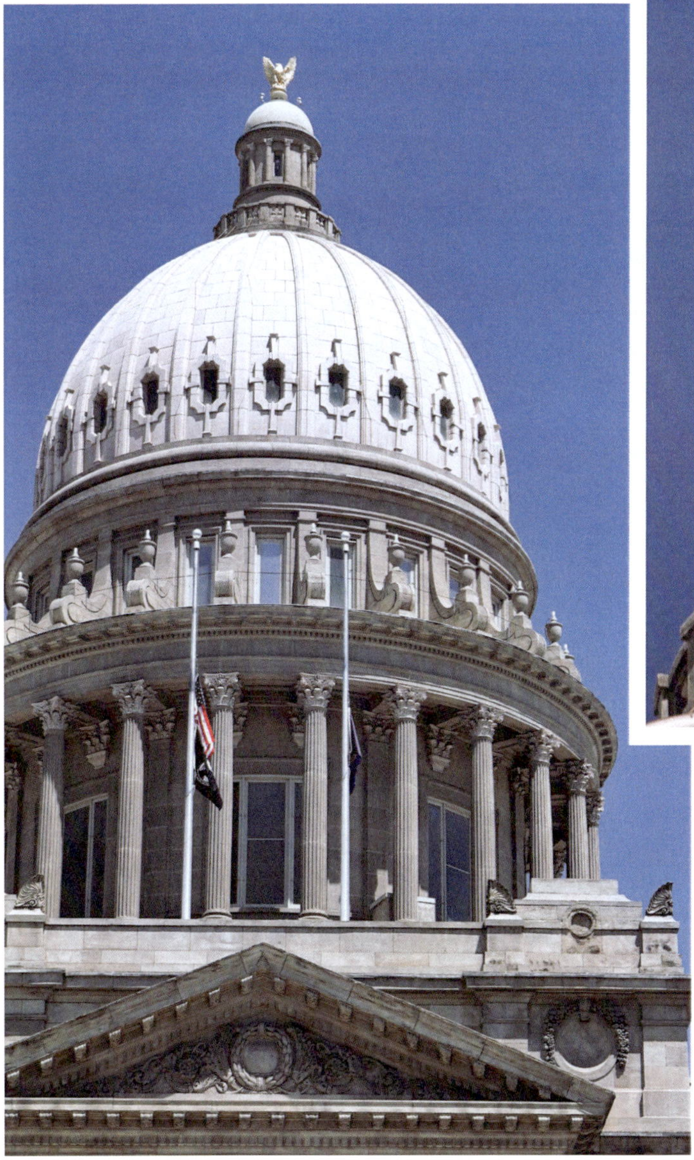

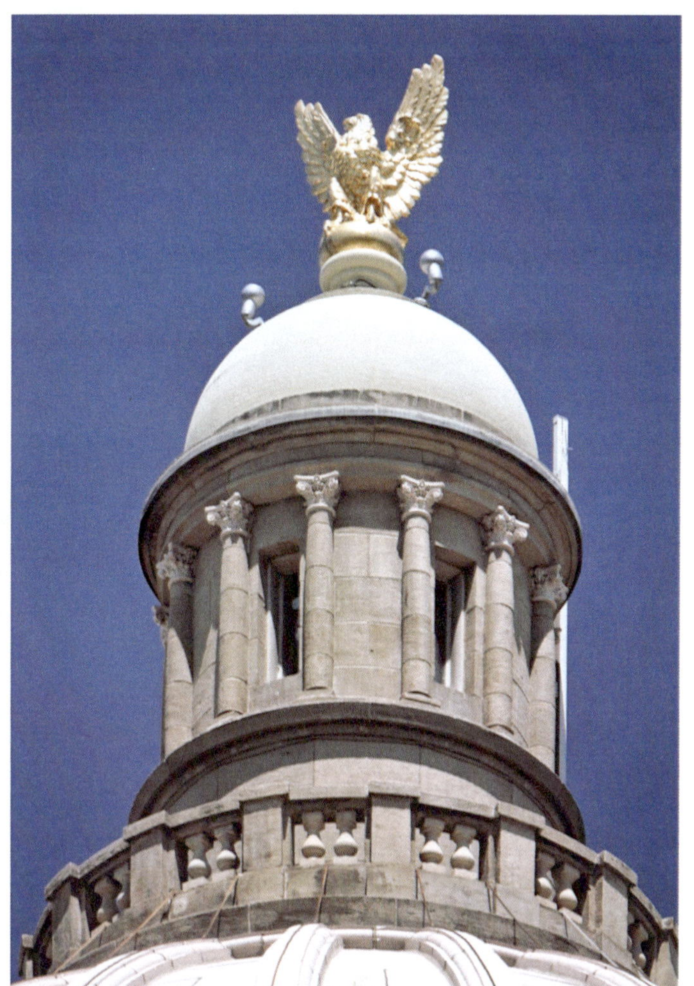

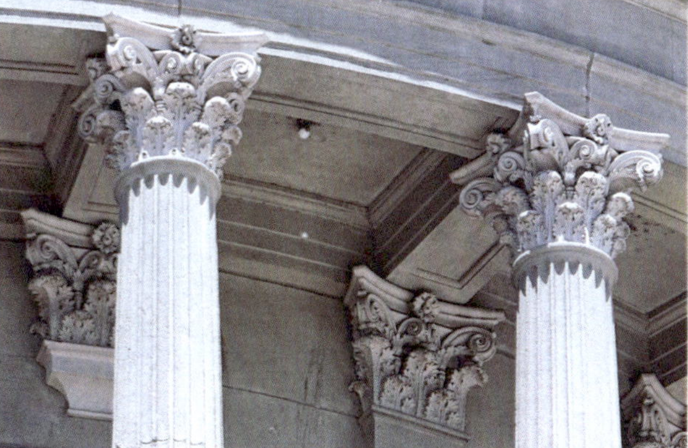

Rotunda Dome

Shining down from the top of the inner dome, called the oculus, or eye of the dome, are 13 large stars which represent the 13 original colonies, and 43 smaller stars, representing Idaho's admission as the forty-third state in the Union.

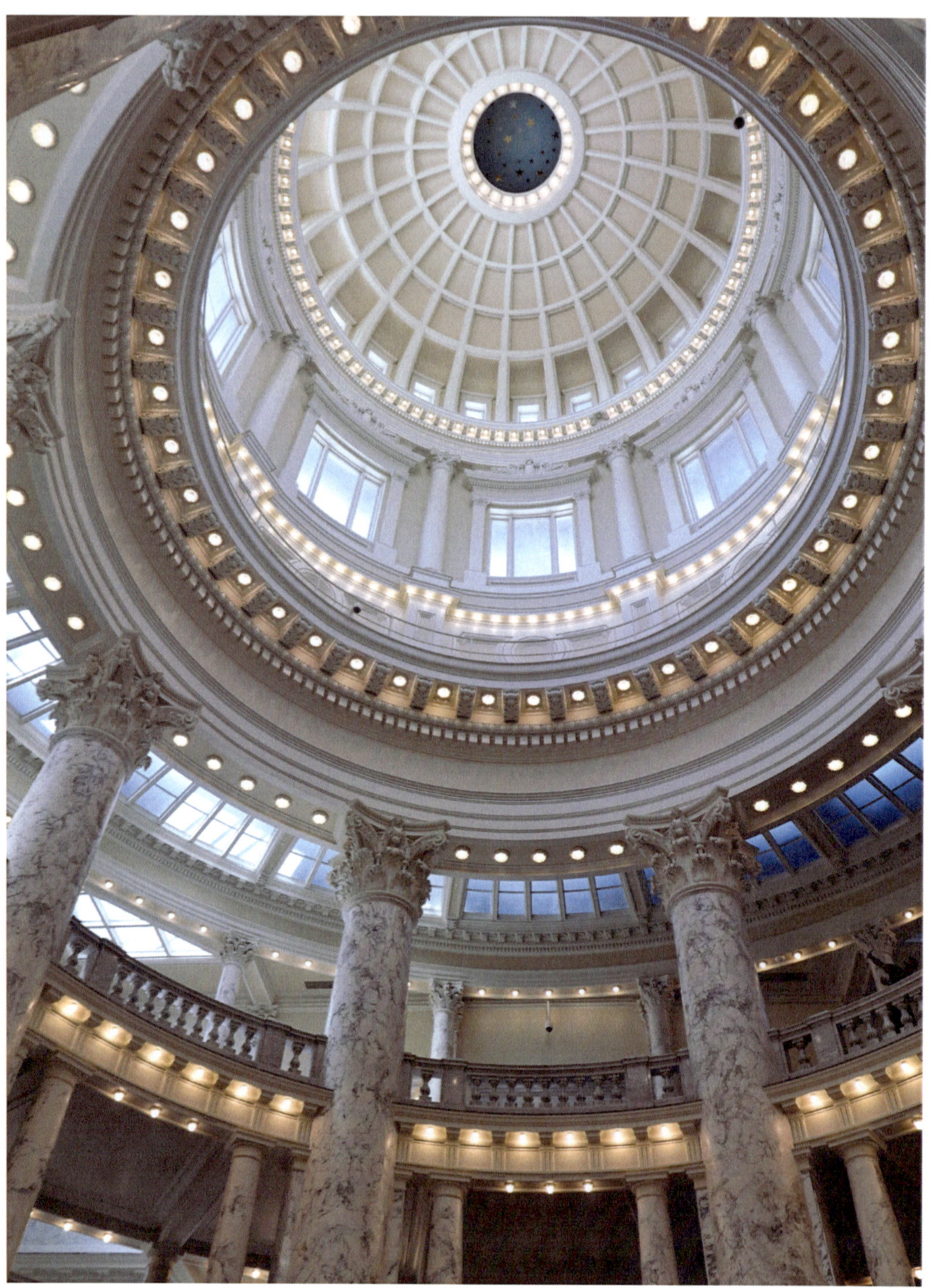

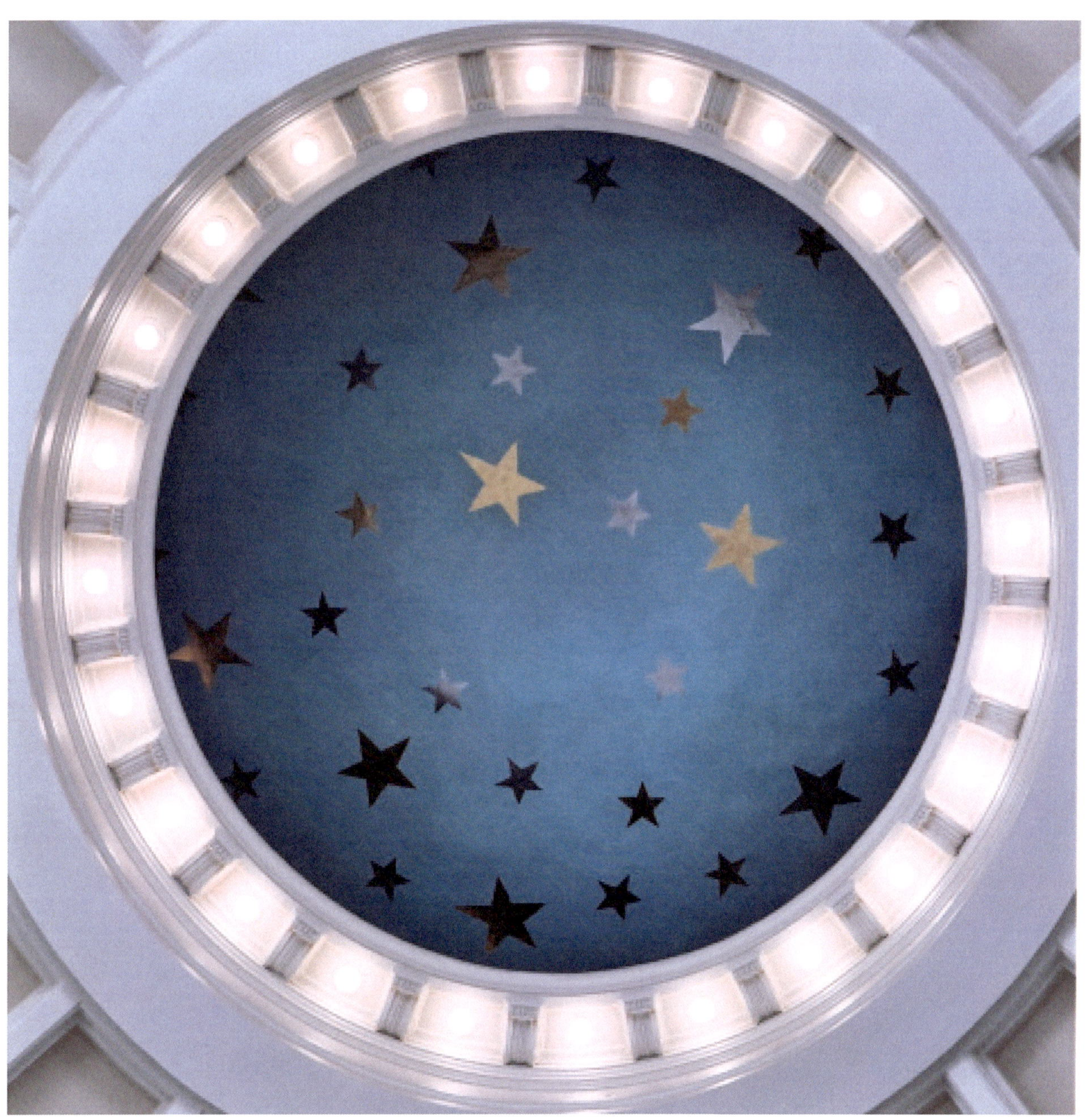

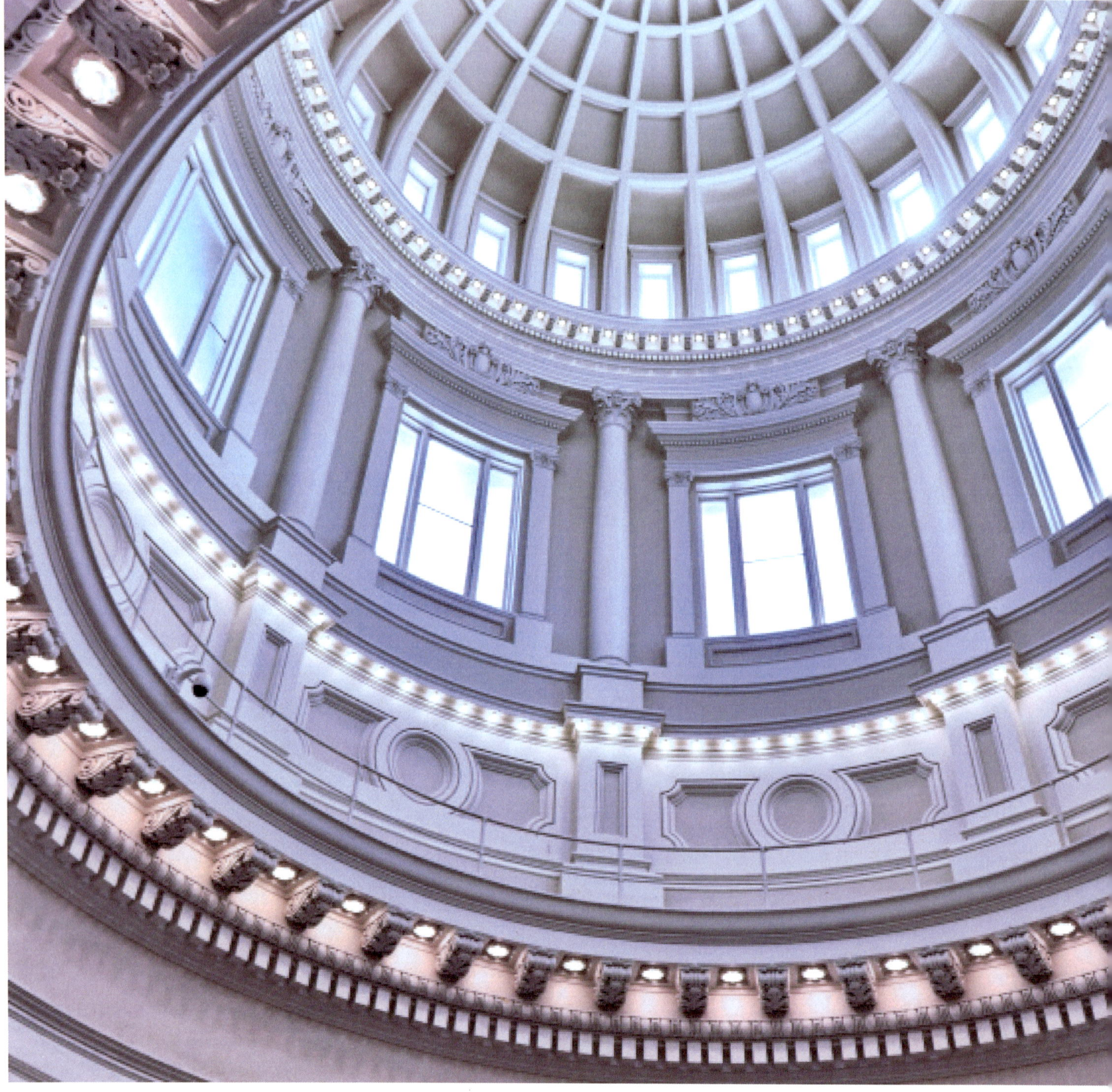

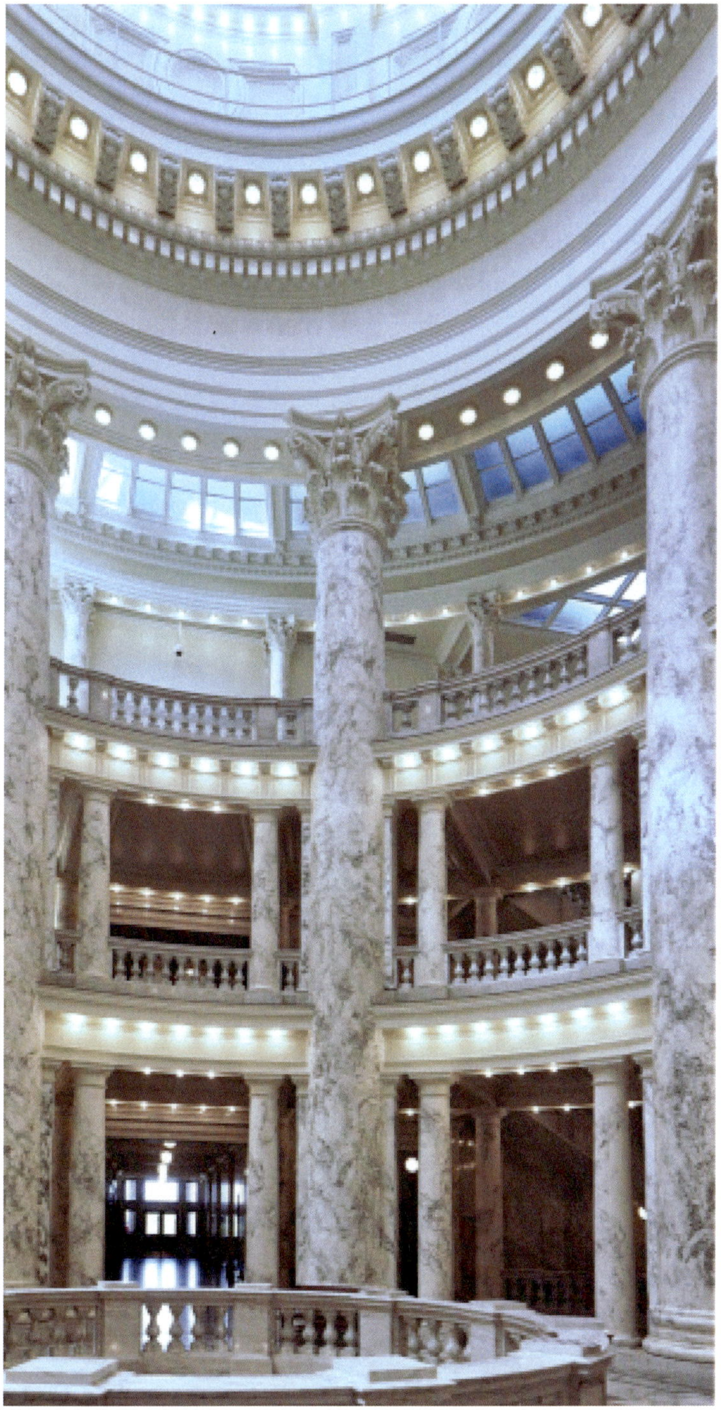

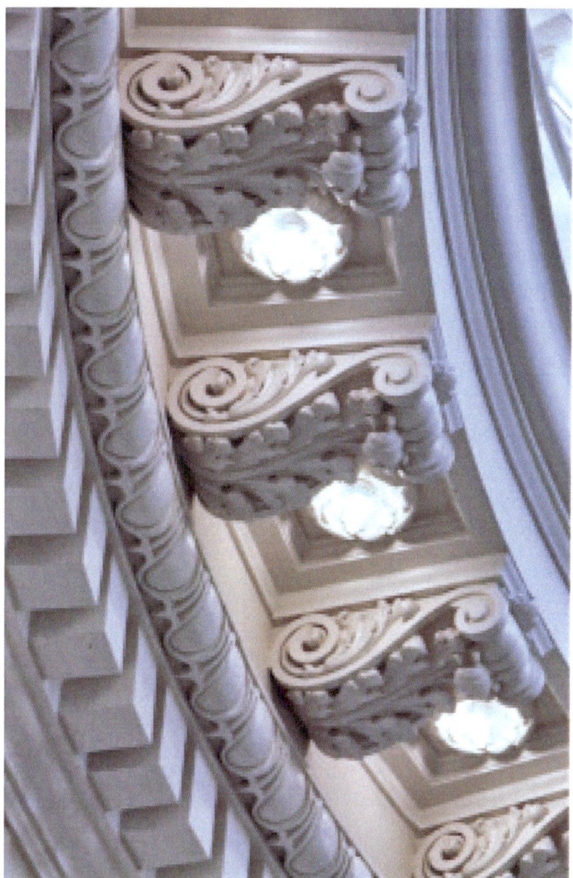

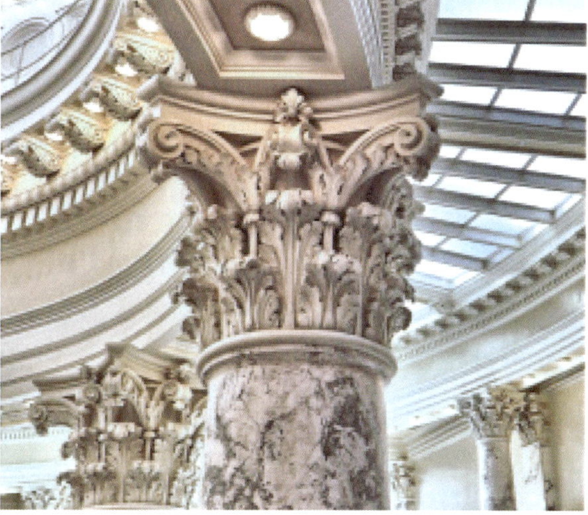

Scagliola, Marble Columns

Eight 60-foot-high columns support the dome and surround the gray, black, and red compass rose medallion on the first floor.

The massive columns are not solid marble, but are steel with a finished surface composed of scagliola -- a mixture of gypsum, glue, marble dust and granite dyed to look like marble. Scagliola originated in Italy during the sixteenth century.

Four types of marble were used for the Capitol's interior: red from Georgia, gray from Alaska, green from Vermont and black from Italy.

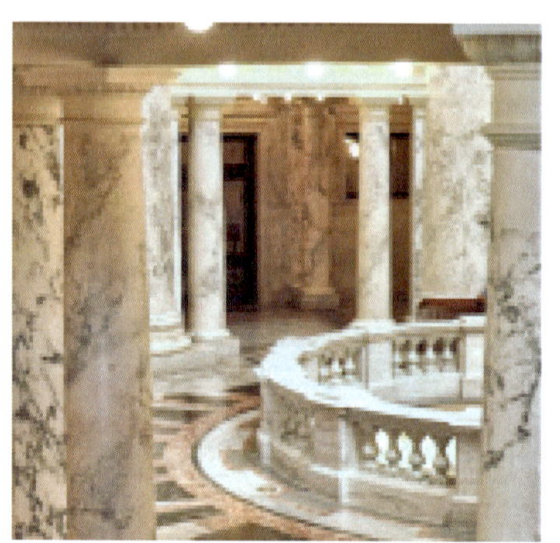

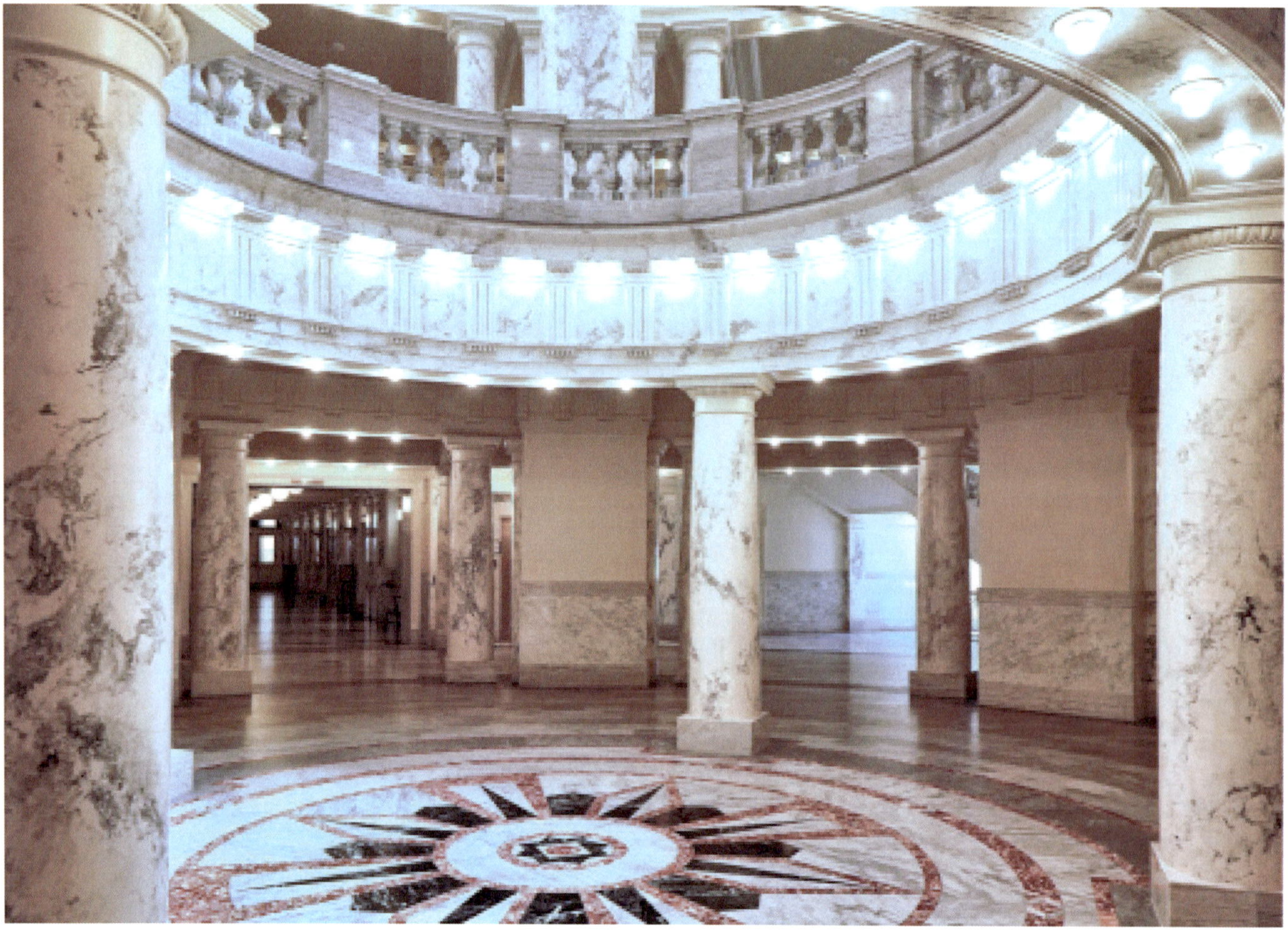

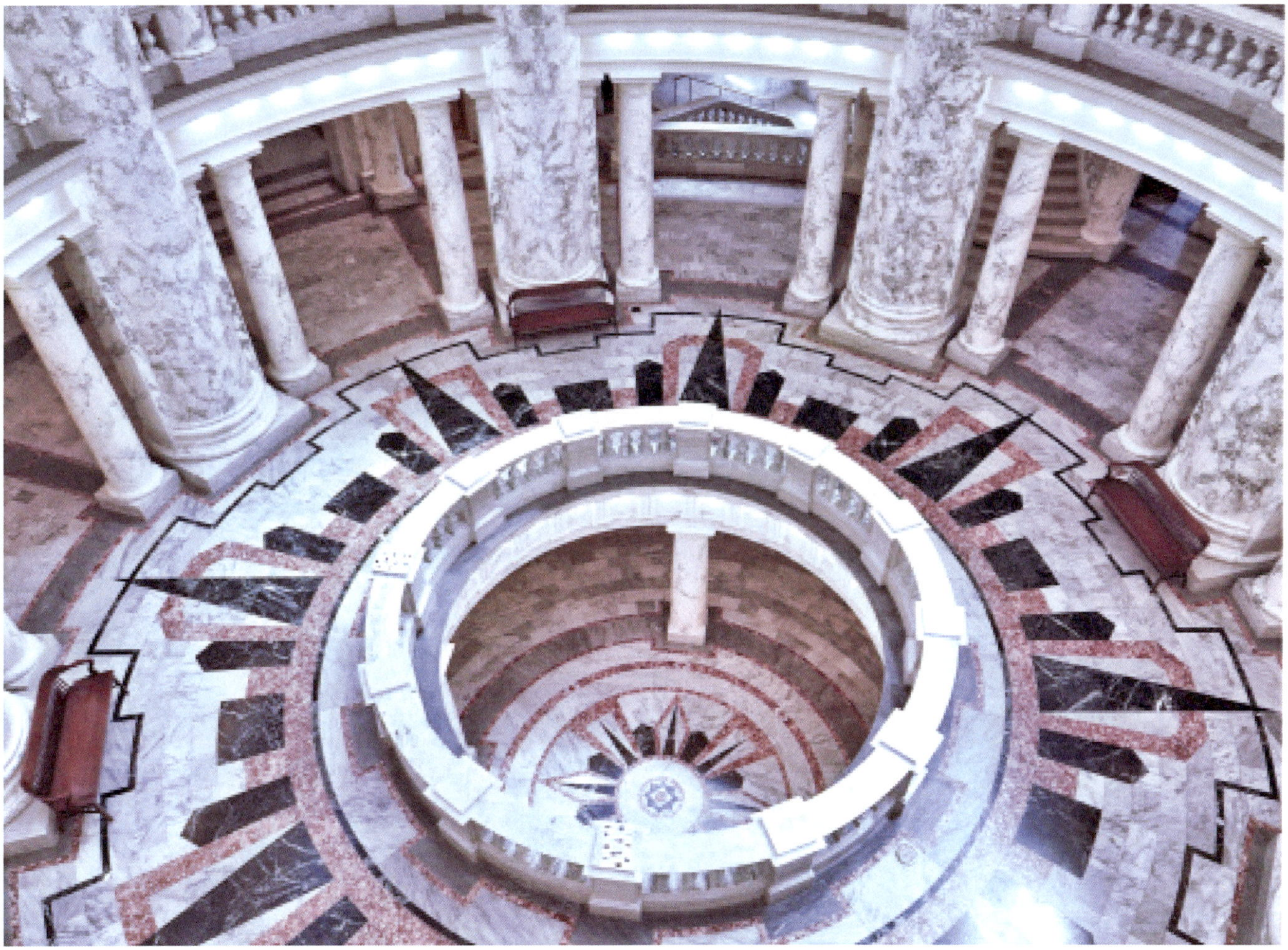

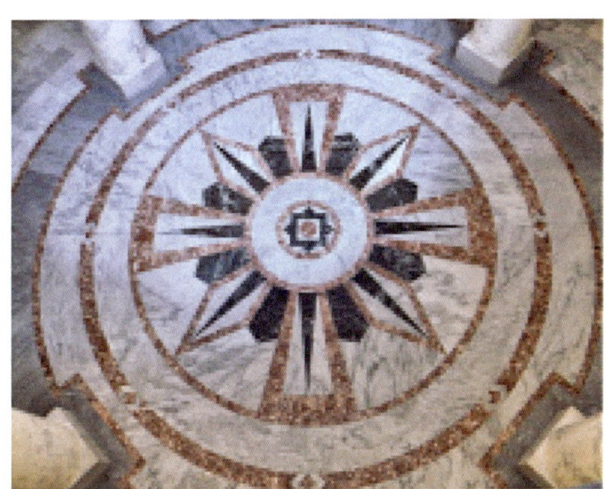

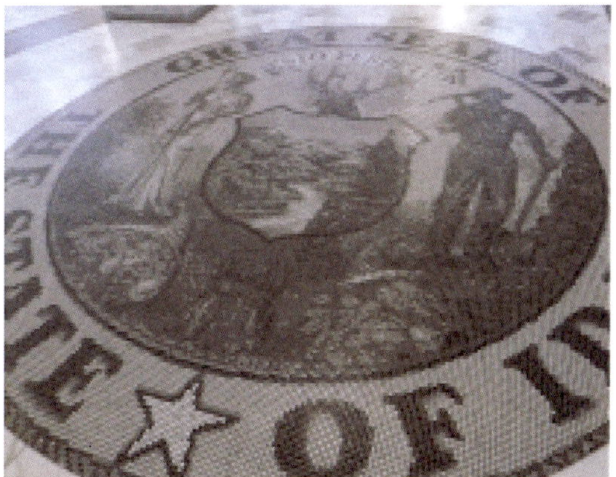

The Idaho state seal is depicted in a glass mosaic on the ground level floor below the center of the rotunda.

Grand Staircase

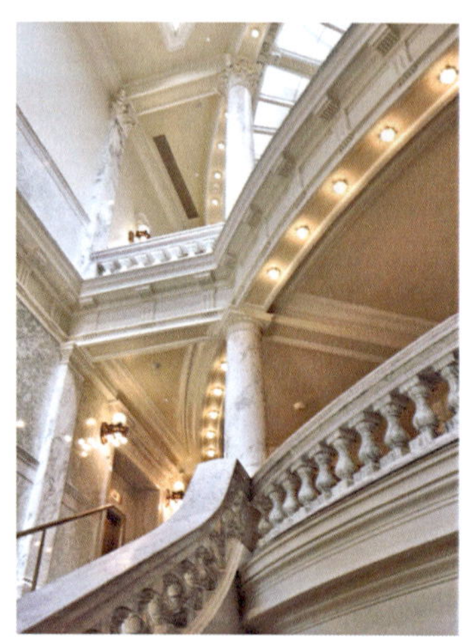

Located on the north and south side of the rotunda, the grand stairways display the carved marble balustrades as well as Brocadillo marble, a greenish white marble with green veins used for the wainscoting and upper wall panels of the staircases.

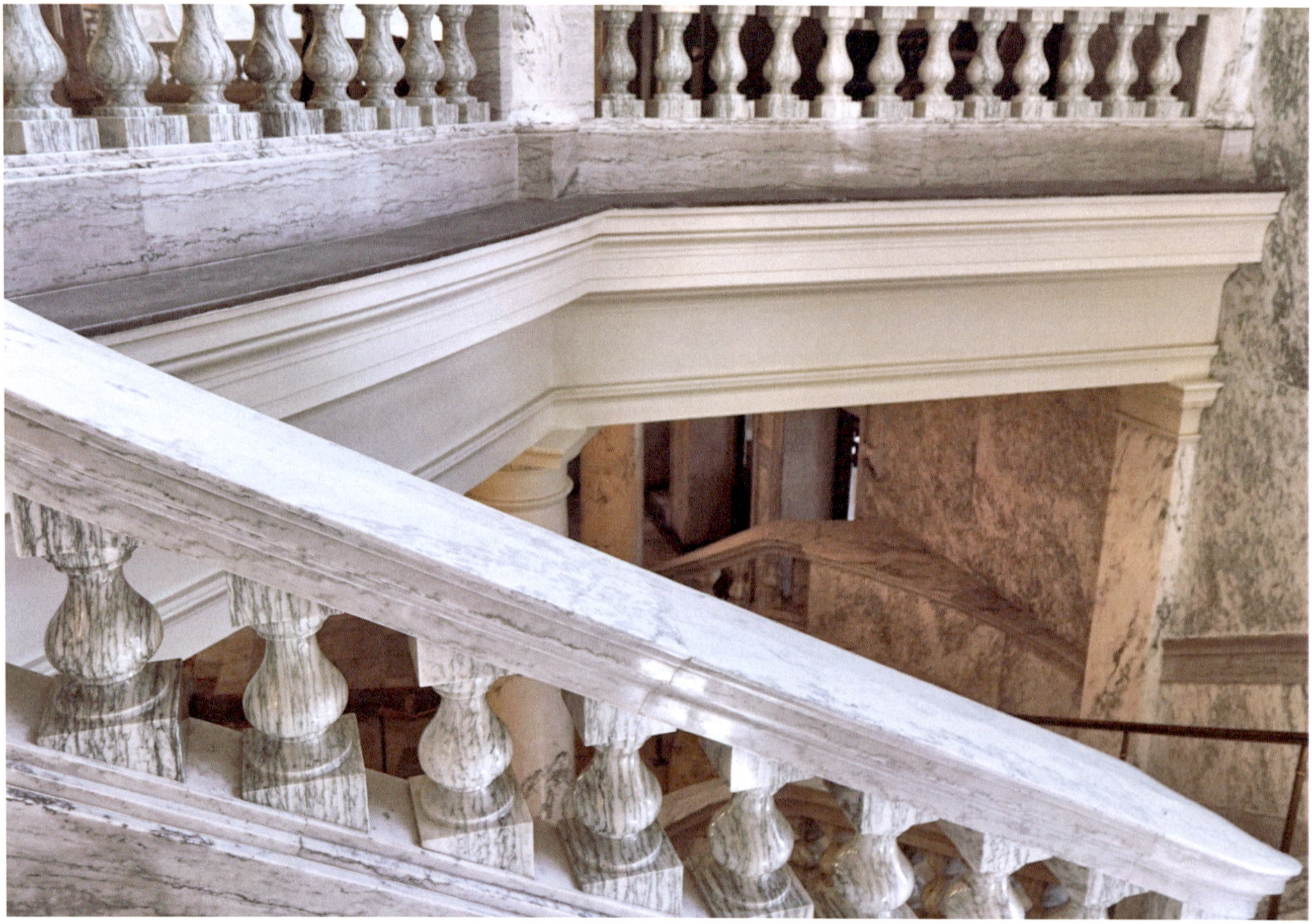

Governor's Ceremonial Office

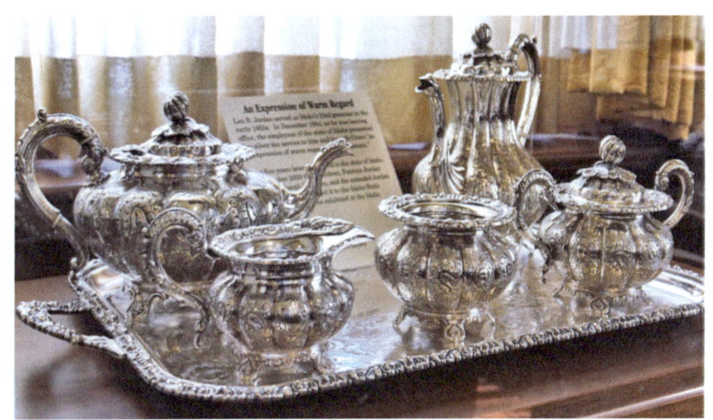

Signing of bills, special receptions and gathers are held in the Governor's ceremonial office.

The roll-top desk, in the background of the photo, has been used by Idaho governors since 1919.

As an expression of warm regard, state employees presented the silver-service to Idaho's 23rd governor Len B. Jordan in the early 1950s. In 2009, his family gifted the silver-service to the state to be exhibited.

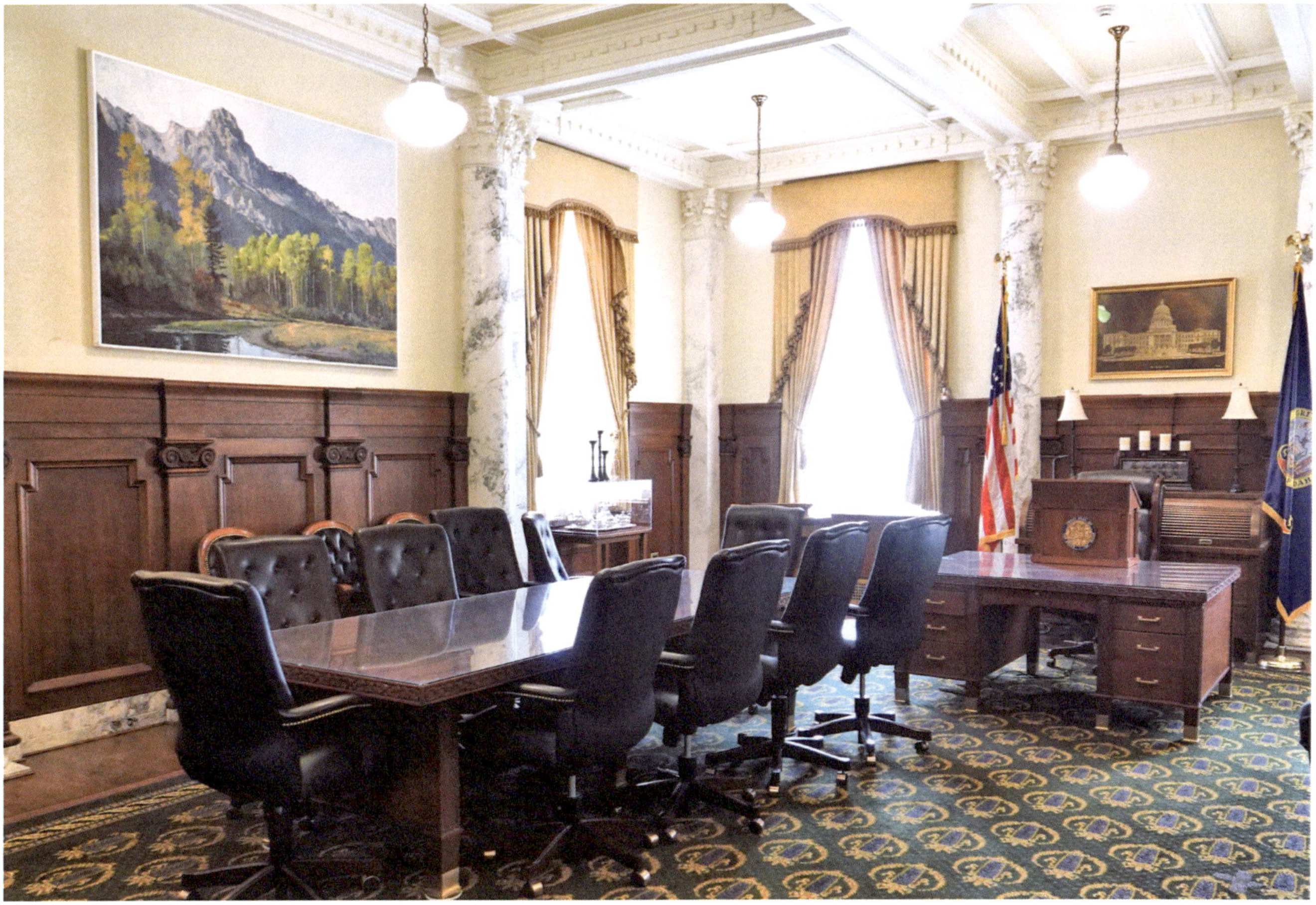

Idaho's legislative chambers are identical in design with glassed, dome ceilings.

There is a slight difference in the molding around the base of the dome. The Senate is more decorative, while the House is modern with circular windows.

Perimeter walls of each chamber were added in the 1970s to improve acoustics. The wall drapes coordinate with the chambers' color scheme which mimics the U.S. Capitol -- red in the Senate and blue in the House.

The furniture in both chambers has been crafted to resemble the original desks.

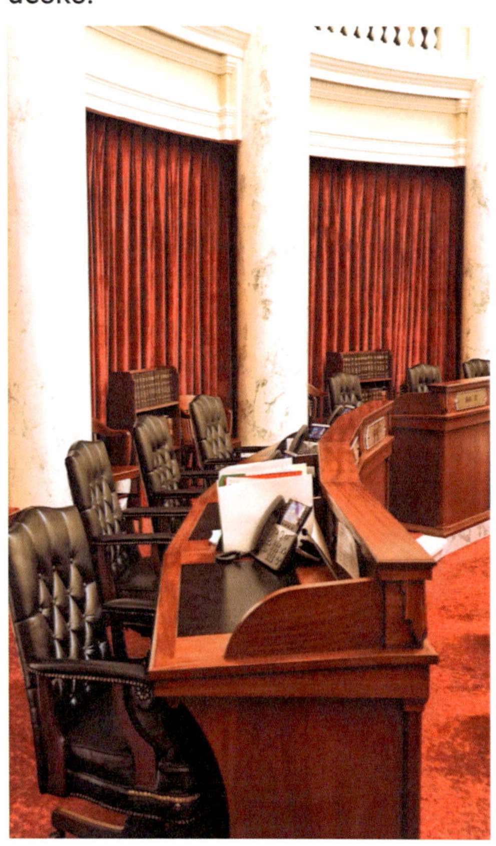

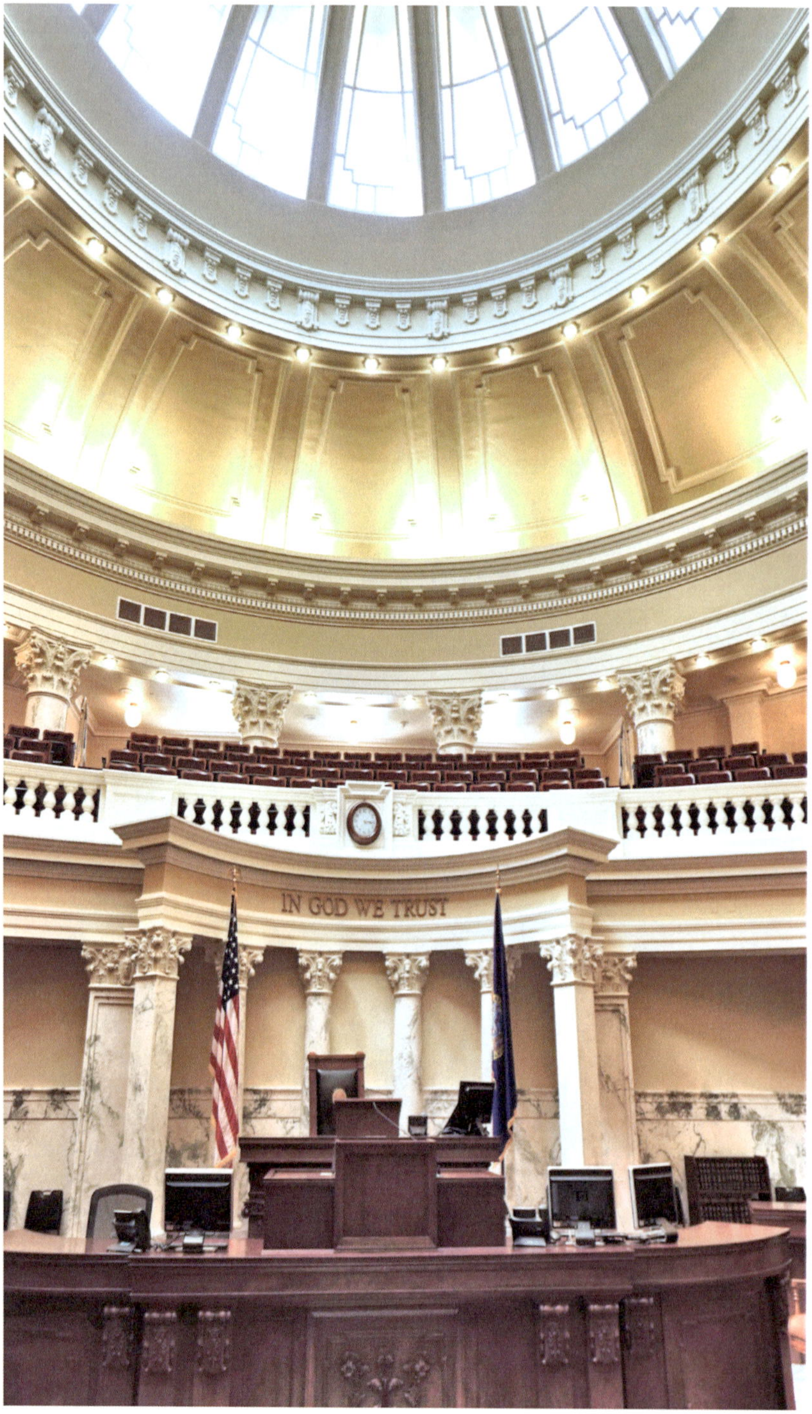

Senate Chamber

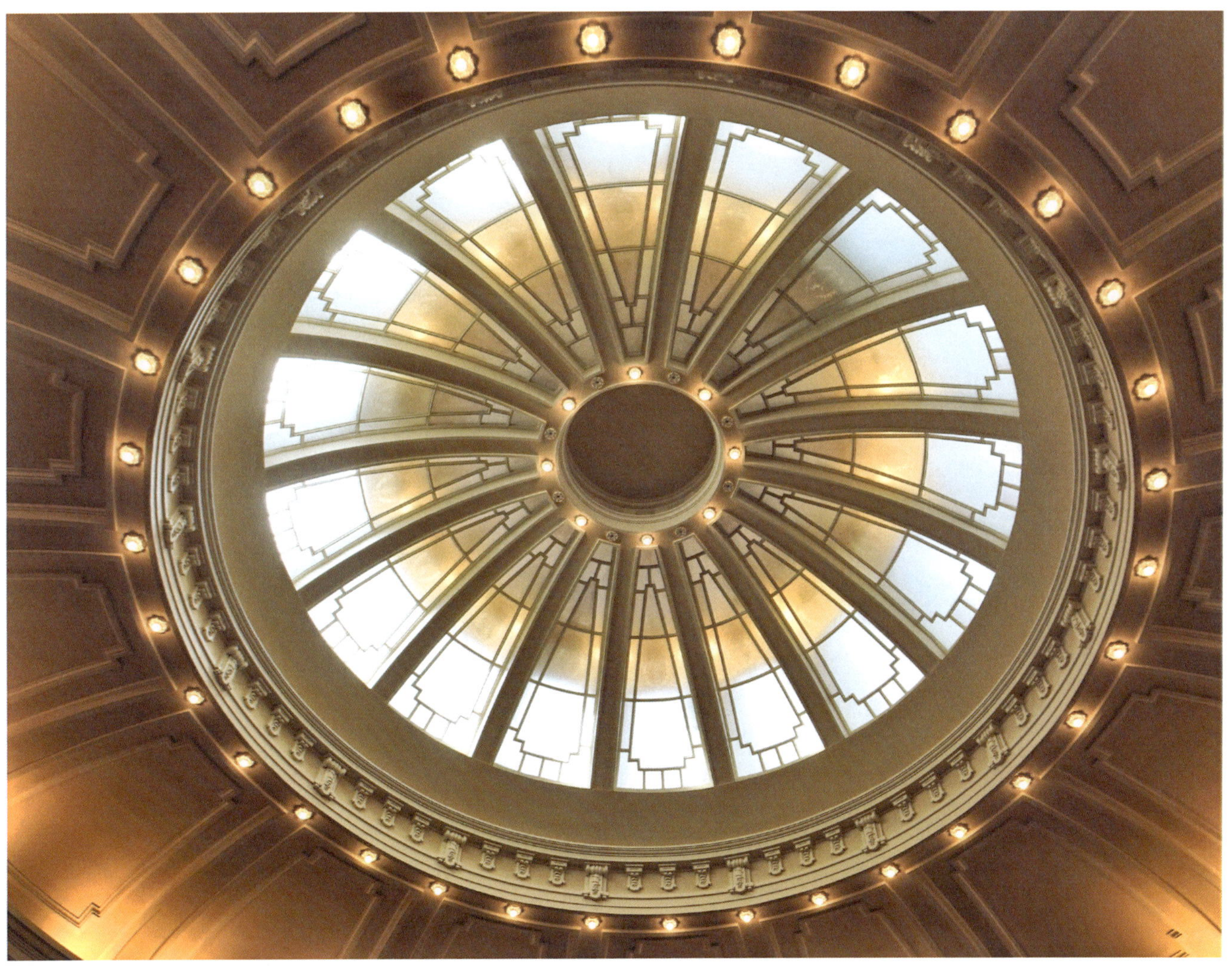

House of Representatives Chamber

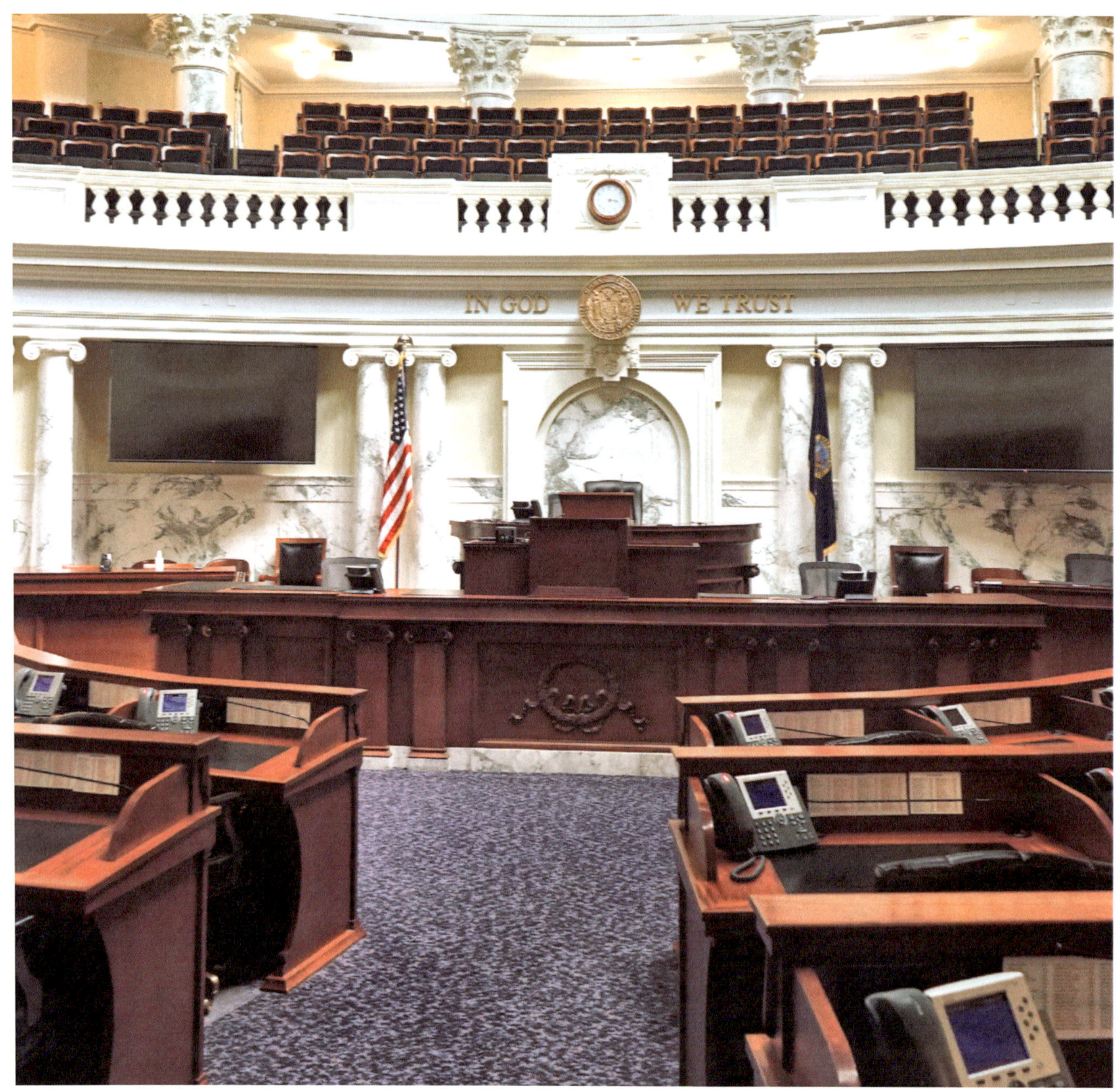

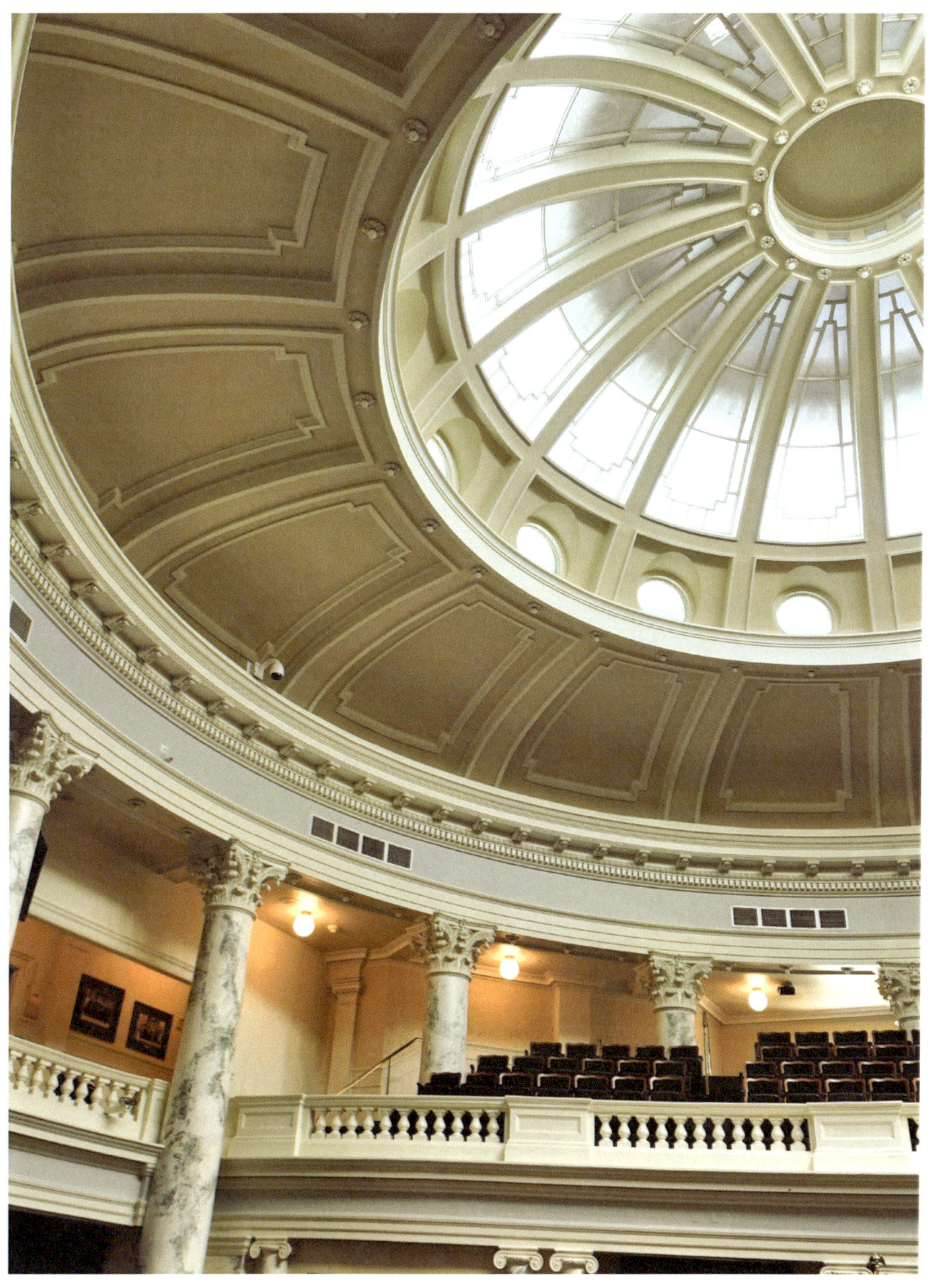

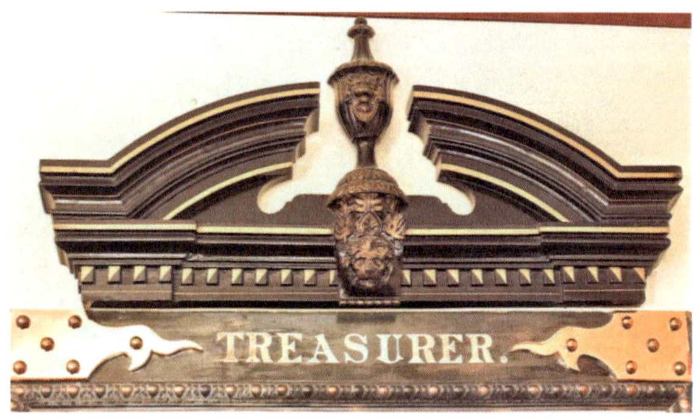

Treasurer Vault

In the Treasurer's office, an original vault still being used today contains a large manganese steel safe made in 1905.

The Manganese Steel Safe Company was founded in the late 1890s as Hibbard, Rodman and Ely Company. At a plant in New Jersey, the company specialized in the manufacture of safes made of manganese steel, including a model called the "cannonball."

The Hibbard, Rodman and Ely Company was so successful with sales of manganese steel safes that it changed its name to reflect the company's success.

The round, double-locked, tightly sealed cannonball safe is still considered one of the most secure models.

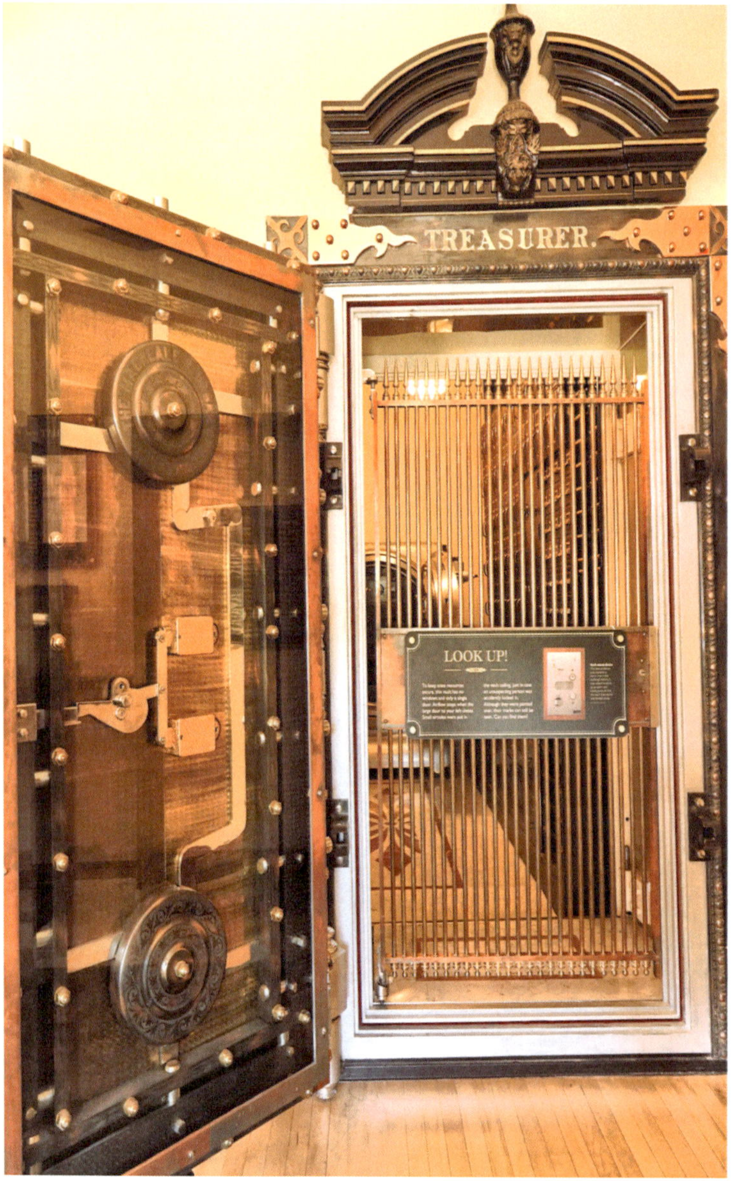

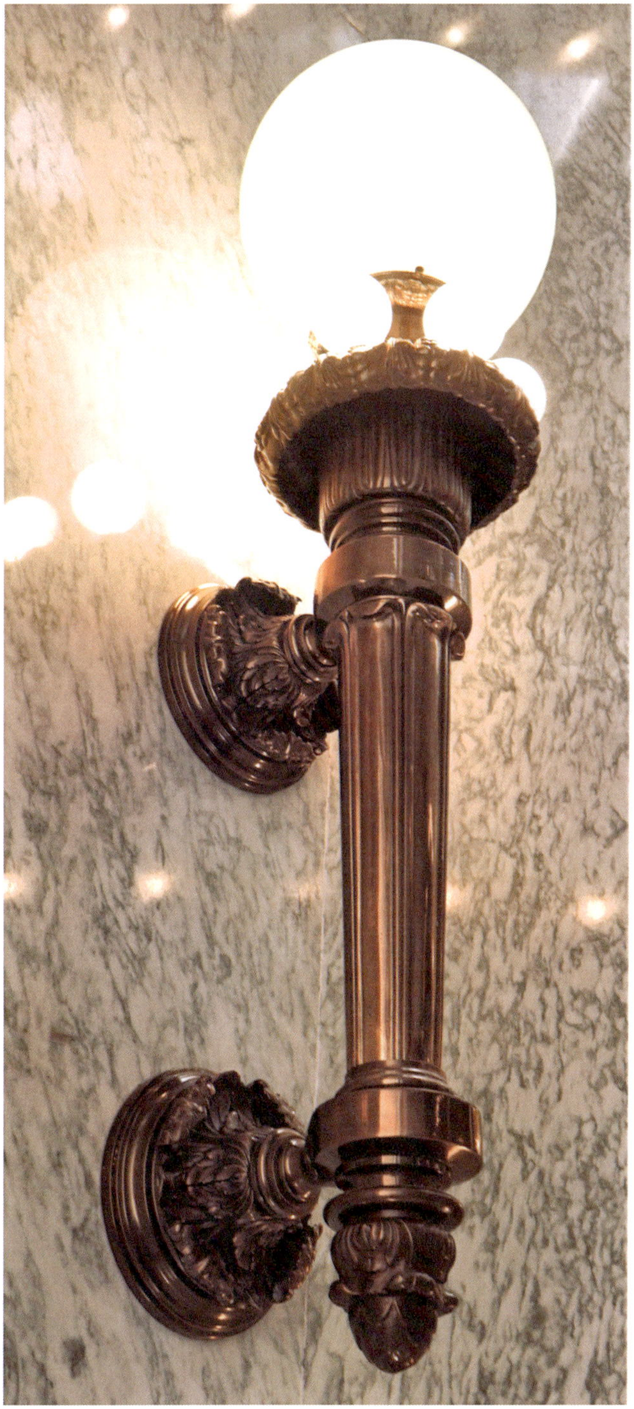

Brass Art Deco

Brass lamps throughout the building are art deco design. Original gas lamps have been converted to electricity and now use LED bulbs.

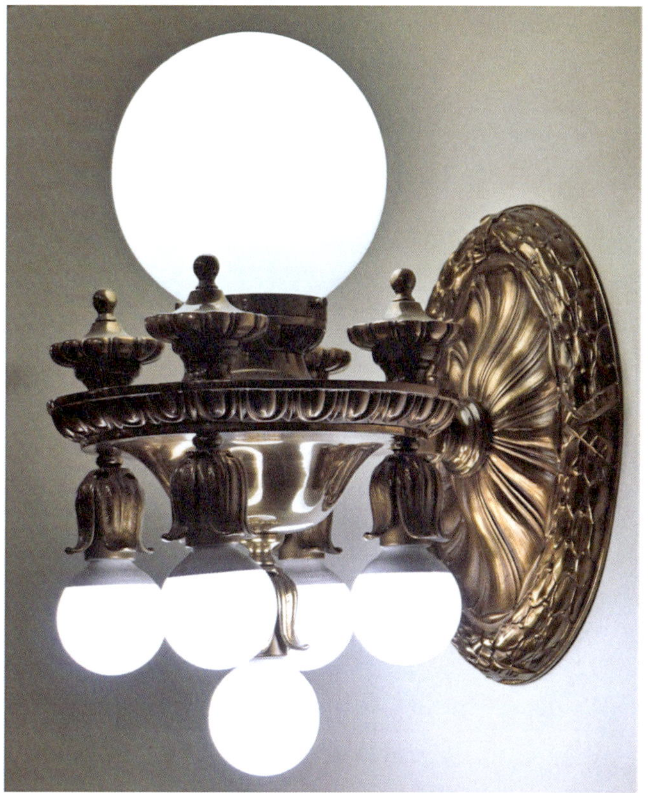

George Washington Equestrian Statue

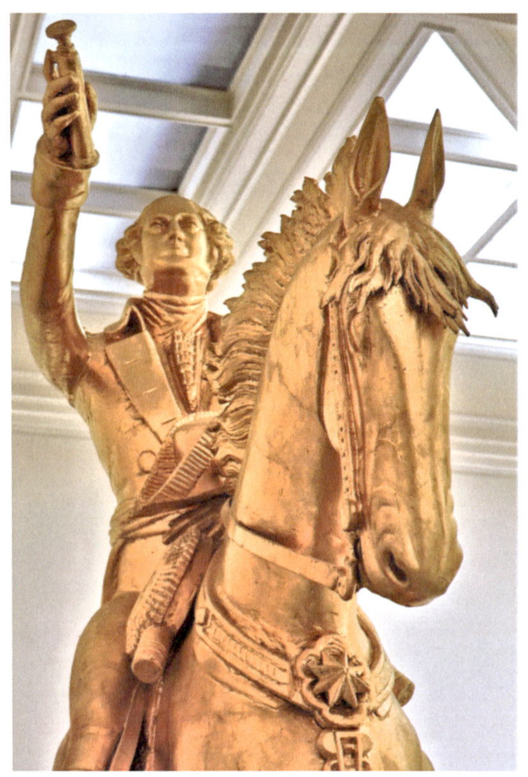

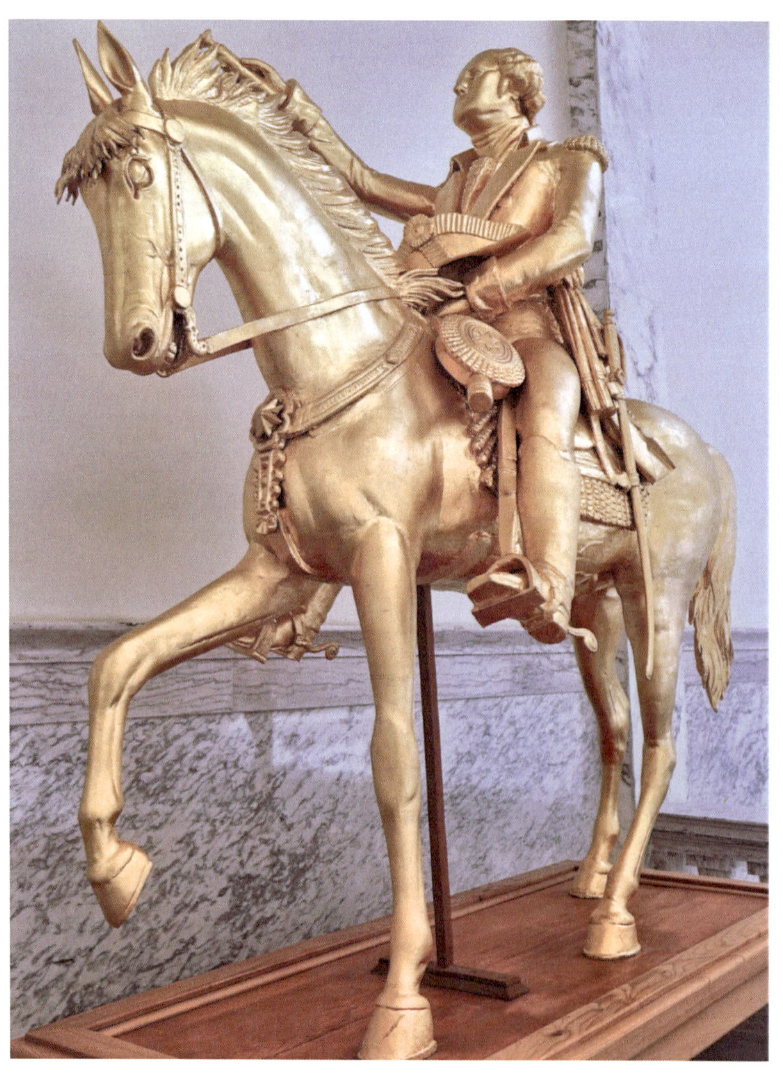

The gold-gilded, yellow pinewood George Washington equestrian statue was carved by Charles L. Ostner for the Idaho Territory and dedicated to its pioneers.

Using a postage stamp of George Washington as a model for the head, Ostner carved at night by torchlight for four years.

The statue originally stood outside the Territorial Capitol in Boise until the current capitol building was built. Then it was restored and moved indoors.

Ostner was born in Germany in 1828. He died in Boise, Idaho, on Dec. 8, 1913.

Winged Victory

This statue is a plaster replica of the original marble statue of Nike of Samothrace found on the island of Samothrace, Greece, in 1863 by a French vice-consul.

The replica is a hollow form plaster cast supported by armature structure.

This statue was part of a larger gift given to Idaho by the city of Paris as a 'thank you' to the United States for its aide in liberating France from Nazi Germany in World War II.

All U.S. states received a train boxcar of gifts from France.

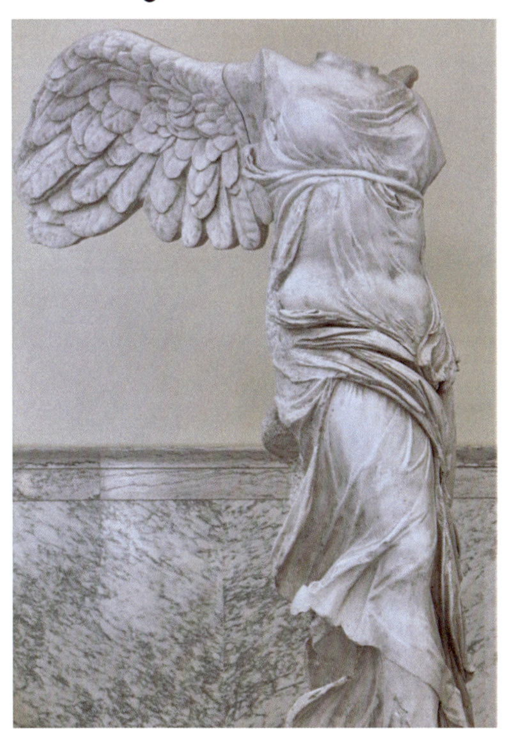

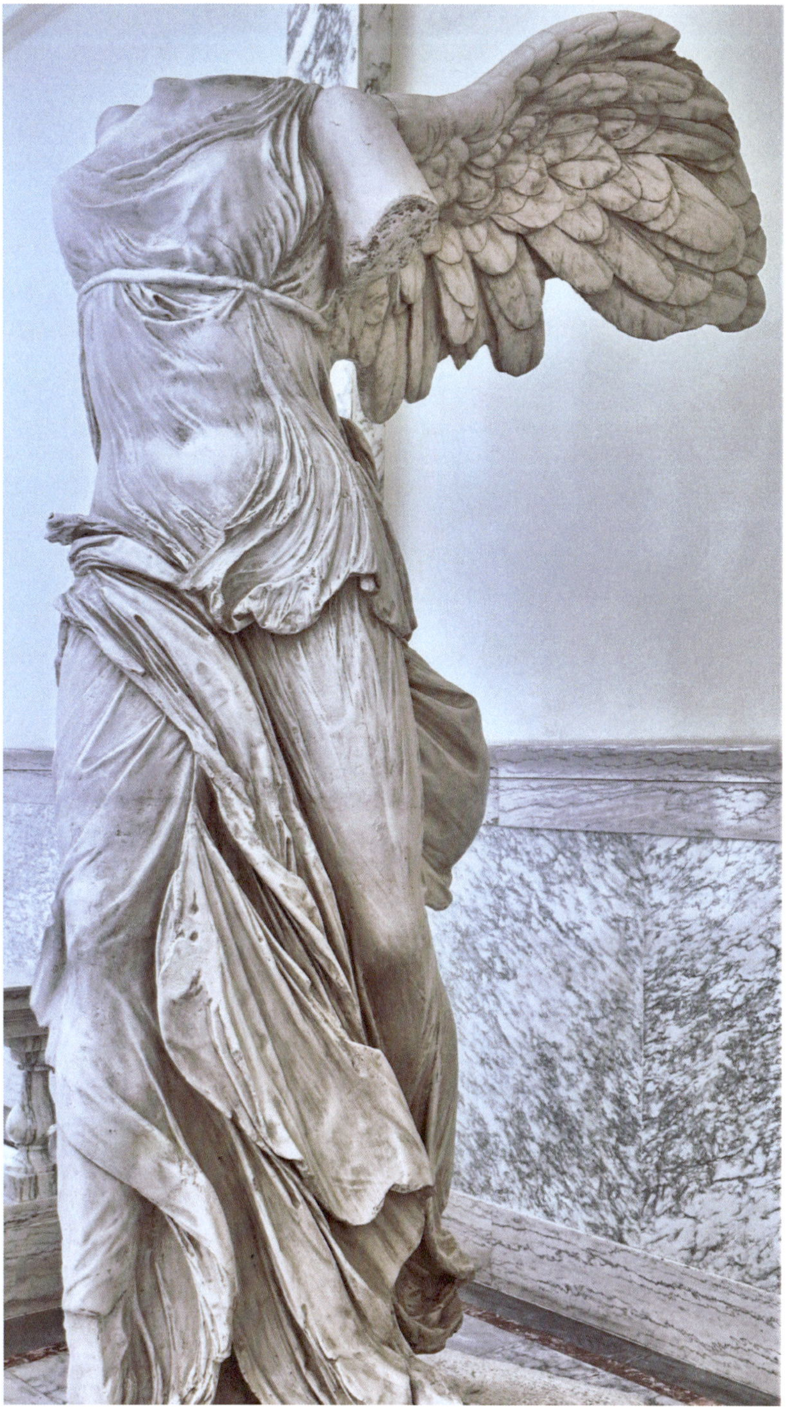

Great Seal of the State of Idaho

The Idaho state seal was originally designed by Emma Edwards Green in 1891.

She is the only woman ever to achieve such distinction in the United States.

The seal was revised in 1957 by Paul B. Evans in order to more clearly define Idaho's main industries, mining, agriculture and forestry as well as highlight the state's natural beauty.

The seal contains the text "Great Seal of the State of Idaho" in the outer ring, with the star that signifies a new light in the galaxy of states.

A woman signifying justice and a man dressed as a miner are located on each side of a shield. The miner represents the chief industry of Idaho at the time of statehood.

The miner reminds us of the chief industry of the State at the time of statehood.

At the center, a shield bearing images symbolic of the State. The pine tree in the foreground refers to Idaho's immense timber interests.

The man plowing on the left side of the shield, together with the sheaf of grain beneath the shield, are emblematic of Idaho's agricultural resources, while the two cornucopias, or horns of plenty, refer to the horticultural.

The elk head rising above the shield symbolizes the state;s game law which protects elk and moose.

The state flower, the wild Syringa or Mock Orange, grows at the woman's feet, while the ripened wheat grows as high as her shoulder.

The river depicted in the shield is the Snake or Shoshone River.

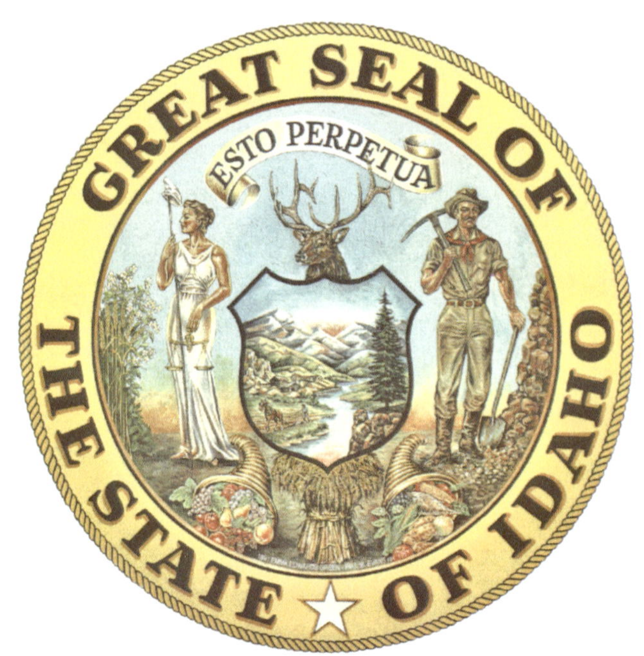

About the Photographer

Jane Moorman describes herself as an adventurer who loves to drive the back roads to see what there is to see.

During her 30-year journalism career, Jane honed her photographic skills as a photojournalist, including covering high school sporting events.

A friend once said, "I wish I could see the world as Jane sees it.

Finding the beauty in things that most of us don't take time to see."

Upon retiring in 2021, Jane decided there is a lot of her native country she had not visited, including each state's capitol, so she began her journey of exploring the USA.

Jane currently lives in Albuquerque, New Mexico, but says her real home is on the road.